AF408416

The Adventures of Timmy & Ace the Dog

by
Michael Gibson

illustrated by
Deni Aris Susanto

Timmy and his best buddy, Ace the Dog, lived out in the woods, with his Dad, Papa Jack and his Mother, Mama Mable.

Timmy and Ace looked out the window of their home. It was a cold and snowy night. Timmy asked Papa Jack, "Papa Jack, why have we never been to town?"

Papa Jack said, "We don't have a lot of extra money, or a way to get there."

Mama Mable said to Timmy, "If you can bring up the "D" in math that you got on your report card, Papa and I will find a way to get you to town."

Timmy went to his bedroom and picked up his math book. He knew that report cards would be sent out in four weeks. Timmy would study every night with Ace at his feet. Ace barked at Timmy saying, "Study hard so that we can both go to town."

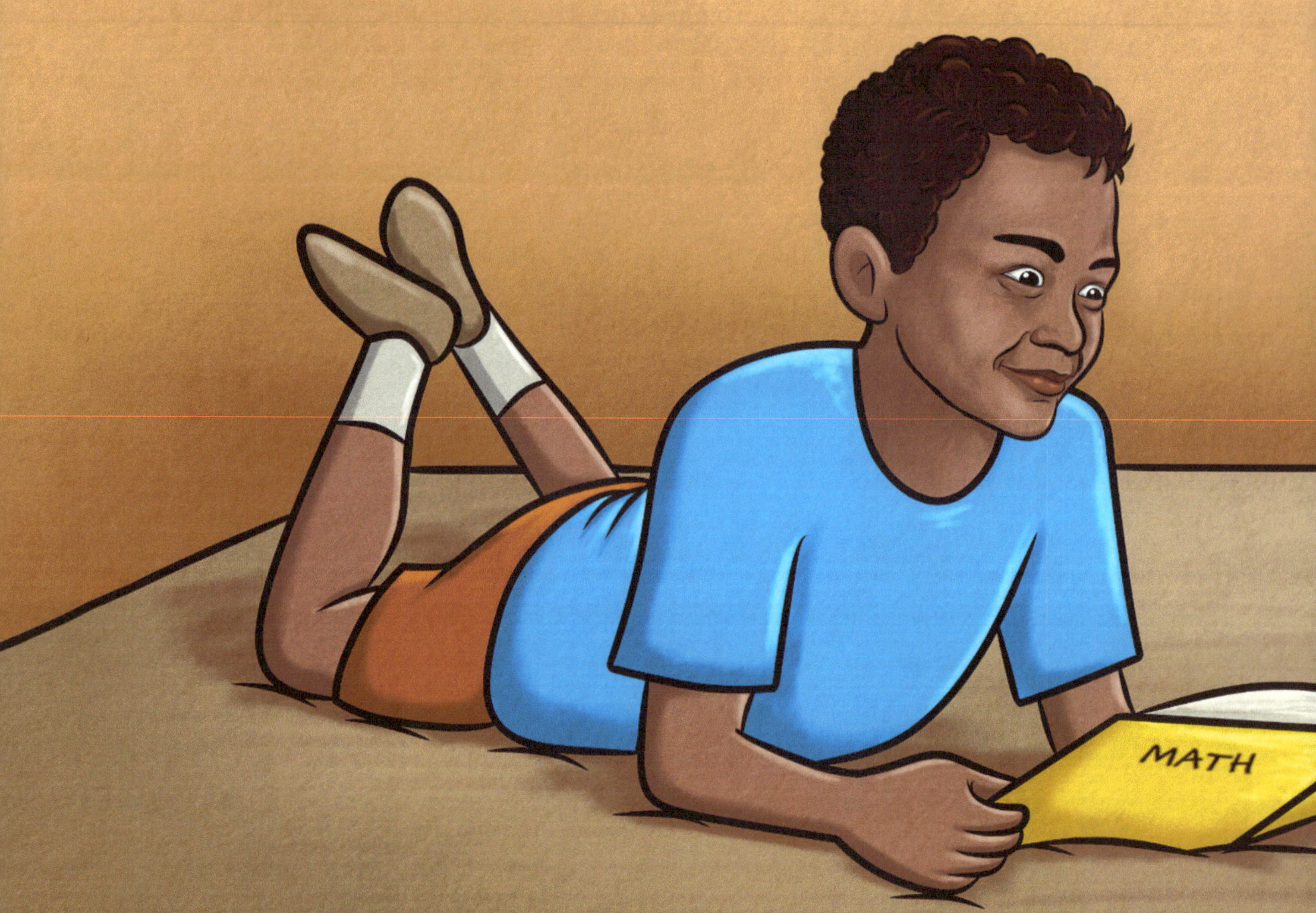

MATH
A+

Four weeks later, Timmy said to himself, "the report cards should be coming any day now." He grabbed the lunch that Mama Mable had made for him and walked to school. After 6 hours the bell rang and the school day was over. Timmy started the two mile walk to his home and soon stood at the end of his gravelled driveway.

He stopped short of his home and was looking in the picture window. He saw Mama Mable, Papa Jack and Ace the dog, standing in the middle of the kitchen. Timmy paused at the front door. His heart was pounding like a big bass drum. He wondered what was going on. Did his report card come today? Slowly he opened the front door. All eyes were on him; Mama Mable yelled out, "Son, you got an "A".

Mama Mable handed him the report card. There were four other classes on Timmy's report card, but he focused on only one, the "A" in math. He dropped the report card and started jumping up and down. Ace started barking and was jumping up and down as well. Papa Jack said, "Be careful, you two look like kangaroos jumping on a trampoline, don't hurt yourselves. Now, we have to find a way to get you to town."

Mama Mable stated,
"I should call Sammy the Stork and see if he has any babies to deliver this month. If he does, maybe you could catch a ride with him." Mama Mable picked up the telephone and called Sammy; and she explained the situation to him. Sammy the Stork said he would check his calenderer and call mama Mable back. "We can also think about getting help from Eddie the elephant."

Timmy said that he would rather go with Sammy, because getting there would be faster than riding on an elephant's back.

Two weeks later, Sammy the Stork called and said that he had a baby to deliver about a mile from their home. It would be a Saturday, and that would be good because school would be out. Mama Mable and Sammy the Stork completed the arrangements. Now she could tell Timmy and Ace what they would need for their trip to town.

Clean warm clothes and Timmy's
special whistle. This whistle looked
like a miniature flute with three
keys. One key was for emergencies.
One key was for contacting mom
and dad and the last one was for
playing the latest computer games
with other kids. Timmy packed a
large duffle bag and placed it by
the front door. Saturday couldn't
come fast enough; it reminded
Timmy of waiting for Santa Claus
on Christmas Eve.

Finally, Saturday had arrived. Around noon, Sammy the Stork
slowly floated from the sky and landed at Timmy's front door.
The weather had changed dramatically; the cold and snow that
had been a problem all month had disappeared and was replaced
by warmer weather; the sky had a glorious red and orange hue,
it was going to be a wonderful day. Mama Mable and Papa Jack
went outside and talked to Sammy. He stated that they would
have smooth, peaceful flight, "a piece of cake," he said.

Timmy grabbed the duffle bag; he and Ace went to give Mama and Papa a hug. Then they went and took their seats on the back of Sammy the Stork. Sammy slowly rose to the sky. Mama Mable and Papa Jack waved to Timmy and Ace and they waved back. Sammy and his two passengers slowly rose from the front yard and disappeared from view.

"I hope they will be ok", said Mama Mable. Papa Jack said, "I'm sure they will be fine."

"Wow," said Timmy, "It is so peaceful up here and the sky is so blue." Floating through the clouds and the gentle sway of Sammy the Stork caused Timmy and Ace to close their eyes for a brief nap.

"Oh no," said Sammy, "looks like we're going to have to fly through some bad weather."

Timmy and Ace awoke from their short nap to see a very dark sky. Sammy the Stork went from being a gentle sway to a feeling that he was a roller coaster. Up and down he went like a yoyo; he was carried so high and then suddenly dropped. Sammy was also being thrown from side to side. He cried out, "I can't control this anymore." Timmy and Ace were so scared that they could not say a word.

Timmy wanted to scream but it seemed like his vocal cords were frozen and he couldn't utter a sound. Ace was barking so loud it was as if he knew they were going to fall to earth.

Sammy began to spiral toward the ground, all three were terrified. It was just a matter of seconds, Timmy thought, before they hit the ground. Suddenly, Sammy began to straighten out his body; he knew that everyone would be safe. Timmy and Ace got up from where they were sitting and began to do their happy dance. Sammy yelled out; "We're going to make it." The sky began to turn blue. All the signs of the terrible weather conditions that had just occurred were gone and Sammy breathed a sigh of relief.

Timmy looked over at Ace and said, "Ho, ho, ho, off to town we go."

Sammy Stork saw the one huge building that was the town landmark; he slowly headed in that direction.

Night-time was approaching and the lights from the
street and the shops would soon be turned on. The town
itself appeared to be clean and well kept. The Neon shop
signs had an atmosphere of fun and happiness.

Sammy touched down landed not too far from the town landmark. Timmy and Ace were preparing to leave when Sammy said, "wait you two. Have fun, I'll pick you up in two hours. Just watch out for the mean Marshmallow Men."
PARK

"Who are the mean Marshmallow Men, Timmy asked?" Sammy stated they were three big marshmallow shaped and colored monsters, with red fangs and coal black slanted eyes. They were known for beating up and being mean to people.

"If you happen to see them, turn on a switch." There were switches at the bottom of each streetlight within the town. These switches had the sole purpose of alerting Lenny the Lion, that the Marshmallow Men were in, or on their way to town and Lenny was the town protector.

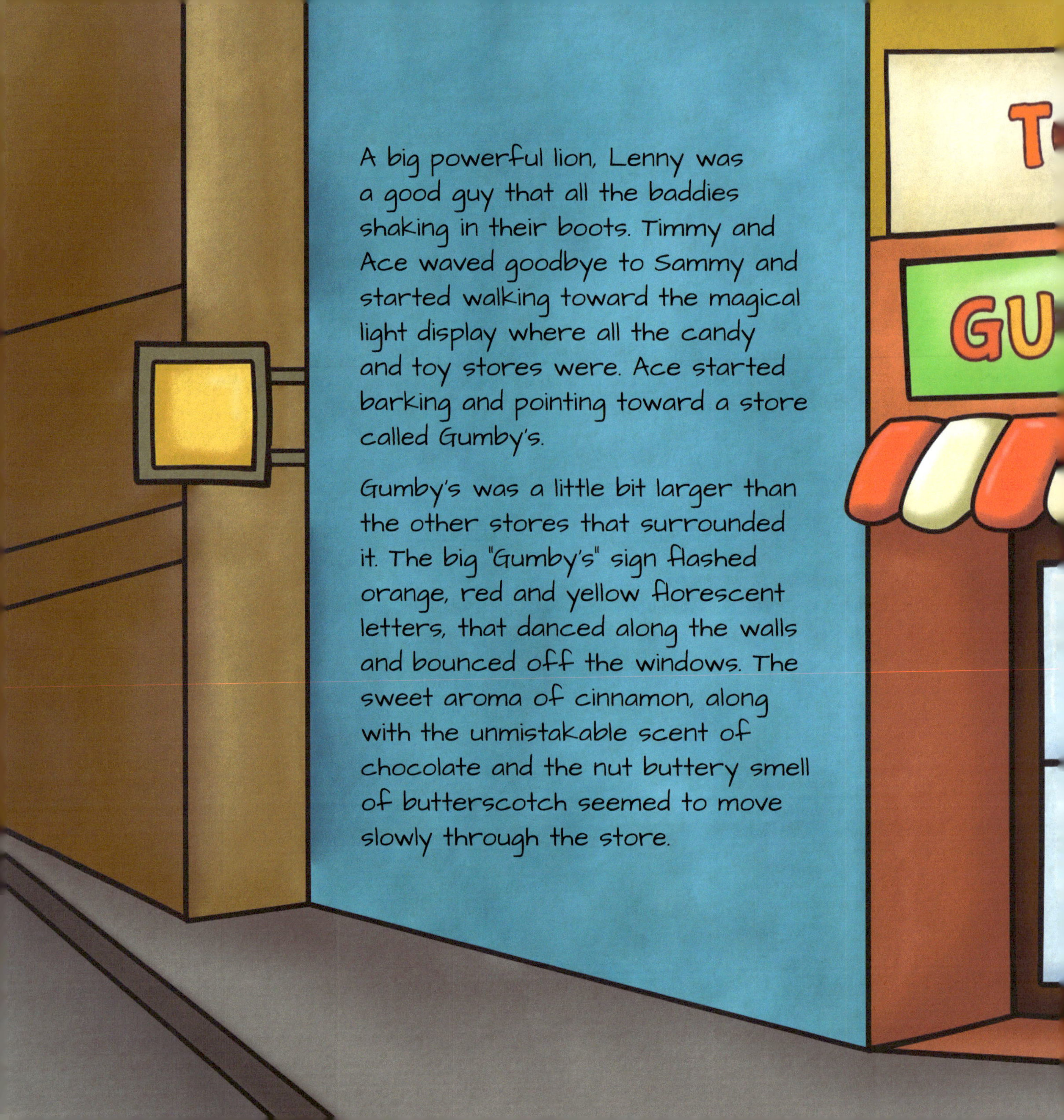

A big powerful lion, Lenny was a good guy that all the baddies shaking in their boots. Timmy and Ace waved goodbye to Sammy and started walking toward the magical light display where all the candy and toy stores were. Ace started barking and pointing toward a store called Gumby's.

Gumby's was a little bit larger than the other stores that surrounded it. The big "Gumby's" sign flashed orange, red and yellow florescent letters, that danced along the walls and bounced off the windows. The sweet aroma of cinnamon, along with the unmistakable scent of chocolate and the nut buttery smell of butterscotch seemed to move slowly through the store.

'S
BY'S
CANDY

Timmy saw Star Wars X-wing fighter jets and the life-sized figure of the furry Wookie, Chewbacca. "Wow", said Timmy, "I'd like to have either one of these in my playroom. Or both"

Ace spotted a large bronze dog bone that had the aroma of fresh beef and chicken. He barked, as he imagined the dog bone outside his indoor dog house.

An announcement came over the store intercom that the store would be closing in fifteen minutes. Timmy said, "We'd better leave and alert Sammy the Stork to pick us up." Timmy and Ace both had a feeling of happiness and excitement about visiting the town for the first time. As they exited the store the cool air hit their bodies. Timmy said, "It looks like the cold weather will be here before we know it." Ace barked, "Yes" in agreement.

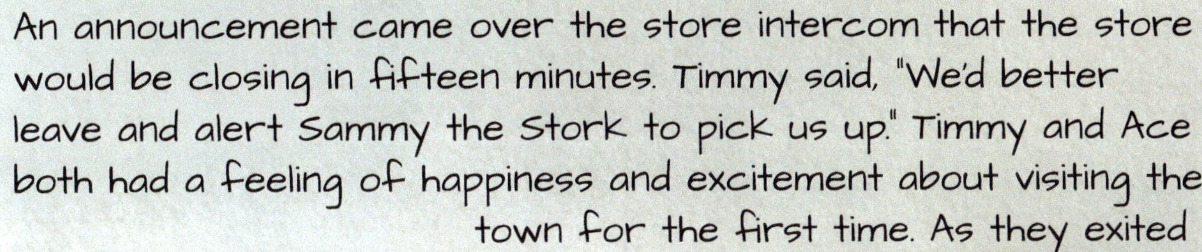

Timmy looked at the horizon and saw what appeared
to be a big white cloud. Ace barked and appeared
to be uneasy as this "Cloud" began to move
quickly in their direction. When Timmy
was able to see clearly, he saw
red fangs and the coal
black eyes. It wasn't a
cloud at all, but
the three

dreaded Marshmallow Men
who were moving swiftly and
steadily toward them.

"Run" said Timmy, as the
Marshmallow Men began
to bear down on them.
Timmy and Ace began to
run as fast as they could.
Ace was well ahead of Timmy,
who didn't see the crack in
the pavement. He tripped and wound
up face first, flat as a pancake on the hard
surface.

Ace watched in horror, as one of the Marshmallow Men jumped in the air and was about to pounce on Timmy before he got up. Suddenly, out of nowhere, a brown blur flew between Timmy and the Marshmallow Man. This blur stopped instantly and began to rise up on hind legs, towering over the Marshmallow Man, it was Lenny the Lion.

Lenny let out a mighty roar, his nostrils were flaring and his eyes were blood red. Lenny had a very mean look on his face as he addressed all of the Marshmallow Men. Lenny said, "You are not welcome in this town. If I ever see you here again, there will be serious consequences."

The Marshmallow Men began to shake and shiver like a freshly made bowl of jello. They began to run as fast as they could in the same direction that they came from.

Ace ran up to Timmy and Lenny. He barked, "That was close, thank you Lenny."

Timmy wiped the sweat from his forehead, still shaken from the close call he had experienced. Lenny said, "You'll never see them again" and he began to leave the area to continue in his role as town protector.

Timmy and Ace walked over to where Sammy the Stork was supposed to pick them up. "Wow, do we have a story to tell", said Timmy. "Yes we do," barked Ace. "Here's to new adventures," said Timmy, "I just hope the next one isn't so scary."

Royalty Kingdom
Creations